Anonymous

In Memory of Mary L. Carter

Anonymous

In Memory of Mary L. Carter

ISBN/EAN: 9783337063122

Printed in Europe, USA, Canada, Australia, Japan

Cover: Foto ©ninafisch / pixelio.de

More available books at **www.hansebooks.com**

In Memory

OF

MARY L. CARTER

BORN AUG. 22, 1836
DIED NOV. 16, 1895

Printed for her Children and Grandchildren
and those who loved her.

NEW YORK
1896

The blessing of her quiet life
  Fell on us like the dew,
And good thoughts where her footsteps pressed
  Like fairy blossoms grew.
                                    WHITTIER.

MARY LOUISA BENEDICT was born in Bridgeport, Conn., on the 22d of August, 1836. She was the eleventh generation by lineal descent from Charles Chauncey, the second President of Harvard College. Among her ancestors on the maternal side were Samuel Edwards, who was at the siege of Louisburg, and Lemuel Coleman, her great grandfather, who fought at Saratoga, the decisive battle of the American Revolution.

When she was two years old, the family removed to New York City where the most of her life was spent.

Early in life, she gave her heart to the Lord Jesus and made a public profession of her faith in Him.

Her father, Mr. Jesse W. Benedict, was an eminent and successful lawyer, who, though well versed in law, was still better versed in the gospel of Jesus Christ. Himself an ardent and delighted student of God's word, he sought early to instil into his children, a love of Bible study. Mary was his eldest daughter, and was greatly interested in her father's Bible studies, and loved dearly to hear him expound the word at family worship.

Dr. Cuyler in one of his spicy letters from "Under the Catalpa," in the *New York Evangelist* says: "One of that noble group of useful laymen whom I alluded to in a former article, was the late Jesse W. Benedict, a prominent lawyer. He came to New York from his native town in Connecticut, when he was about twenty, and a friend in his boarding-house urged him to go and hear Dr. Cox in the Laight St. Church. He was converted there and united with that church not far from the time William E. Dodge joined.

Mr. Benedict was a diligent and profound Bible student. He was more familiar with the different 'Codices' of God's Word than many a graduate of our Theological Seminaries."

Miss Benedict was married to Mr. Peter Carter, of the publishing firm of Robert Carter and Bros., on the 25th of March, 1857, by the Rev. William Adams, D.D. in the Madison Square Presbyterian Church.

The young couple went to house-keeping within a fortnight from the day they were married. Mrs. Carter's love of music, both vocal and instrumental, and her bright and happy manner, drew around her a great many young people. She was rarely known to refuse to sing or play at the request of any one interested in music. The hospitality of the little house became well known, and its sweet young mistress grew to be a universal favorite.

Her husband having been born in Scotland, she took special delight in Scottish songs. By careful attention and painstaking effort she learned to sing them almost like a native.

The Teacher's Meetings of Mr. Carter's Sunday School of colored children were held at their house. These teachers were many of them Scotch and enjoyed greatly the social hour after the business meeting was ended.

Mrs. Carter was the life of the evening. The new teachers and the bashful and timid ones were sought out by her and made to feel at home. All felt the influence of her presence.

Every one of her children took part in the work of the colored school at an early age, and were thus taught to live for others.

Her growth in grace and in consequent usefulness was visible to everyone but herself. Clad in humility, she noticed only her failures while others observed her rapid progress in the Christian life.

She was the loving, faithful mother of nine children, to whose nurture and care she gave herself unreservedly and with the blessed results that always follow such devotion. Three of her children were called to be with Jesus in infancy. Of the others, a loving friend writes : —

"To her six children, too, who have gone out into the world to do the work of brave Christian men and women, her life must ever be an inspiration.

" Many parents lament that their children do not early give themselves to Christ. May not this be partly due to a lack in themselves? Mrs. Carter carefully trained her children to habits of earnest prayer ; she herself not only prayed for them but with them ; she taught them that the service of Christ was a glad, joyous service, and that it was fitting they should acknowledge their Master before their associates and she had the great happiness of seeing them all early enter, one after another, upon a Christian life."

It was a sweet Christian home. Both father and mother endeavored by their example to lead their children in the right way. They made it a happy home by their kindly hospitality. Strangers were always welcome. Ministers and missionaries, the poor as well as the rich, felt themselves part of the family while they tarried. Young men in boarding-houses were invited to Sunday night teas and enjoyed the singing hour that followed.

A missionary of the American Board, writing from a distant land says: "I shall never forget how, many years ago, she made me, an awkward girl, have such a beautiful visit at Lake Mahopac.

"The last time I was in America, I went often to the City and it always seemed to me that the sunniest place in New York was 330 West 28th Street where dear Mrs. Carter was sure to be at home and as sure to treat me, with her genial hospitality, as if I belonged to her."

She was pre-eminently a bright Christian. She breathed an atmosphere of sunshine, and her ringing laugh was an inspiration. To the very last, in spite of days of weariness and suffering, she was not only wonderfully patient but cheerful, with a sweet smile of welcome for all who came into her sick room.

As she was one of the most unselfish of women, so as might have been expected, she was one of the most generous. She regularly set apart one-tenth of her income to the work of the Lord. But she often far exceeded this amount in her giving. She was careful to instil into her children's minds that the tenth belonged to the Lord, and others outside of her family were advised to pursue this blessed plan.

While the family were spending the summer in Stockbridge, Mass., many years ago, she became greatly interested in the spiritual welfare of a little colony of Germans who were working in a pulp mill. She procured tracts and testaments in German and distributed them on Sabbath mornings. They were gratefully accepted, and we cannot but hope that at least some of them were blessed to the spiritual good of those to whom they were given. After her death, among some papers was found one written by her in pencil describing these Sabbath visitations.

She says: "The first house I went to I knocked at the door. It was opened by a German. He said in broken English, 'Come in.' I went in and sat down. His wife soon came in. I asked them how long they had been in this country. The man said he had been here three years. His wife had been here twelve, but he could speak better English than she could. He enlisted soon after he came and was in the war sixteen months. I said, 'Then you learned to speak English there.' He replied that he had been in a German regiment where they spoke no English. He had learned to speak English in Stockbridge. I asked him if he went to church. He said he did and could understand a good deal the minister said. I then enquired if they had a Bible. They had one and they showed it to me. It was a German Bible. I told them that I hoped they read it, and they assured me they did. They said they liked the tracts I had given them on the previous Sabbath—that when night came they sat down and read them.

"Next door, the German woman who opened the door to me had her Bible in her hand. She could not speak English, but she could understand me a little. I gave her three German tracts.

"The next door was opened by an American woman. I gave her some English tracts. Her husband was asleep as he had been in the mill all Saturday night. In the next house I was met most cordially by a German and his wife. I asked the man how long he had been in America. He replied in very broken English that it would be a year in December, but 'his Vrow' had only been here one month. I asked him if he had a Bible. He ran and got it. It was a large one. He said it was his 'Vrow's.' 'She bring it from

Faderland.' I said, 'I hope you read it.' He replied, 'Oh yes. Work all day, night read; have time.' I asked them if they could understand the preaching. He said he could a little, but his wife could understand nothing.

"These Germans are all very grateful and I love to visit them."

A few years later at Lake Mahopac where a large number of Italians were at work in constructing a new railway, she found opportunity to do a similar blessed work. For many Sabbaths she gave them testaments and tracts in their own language. During her last summer on earth although a suffering invalid, set aside from active work for her Master, yet her heart went out to others. Sitting on her piazza day after day, she became interested in a band of Italians at work in the road before her house. She sent to New York for Italian tracts and made the eldest of her grandchildren in Bloomfield her messenger to distribute them among the men.

She was gentle and unassuming yet a born leader. In the Scotch Presbyterian Church in New York, she was a most efficient worker in the Home and Foreign Missionary Societies. The same was true of Bloomfield where she afterwards resided and where she died. She was always a ready helper in getting together boxes for the poor Home Missionaries in the West. In one instance, the recipients were to be a colored family, the father a Home Missionary preacher in Illinois.

It became a question whether the usual enthusiasm and generosity would appear in this case. But the magic of her wise leadership triumphed, and this box proved one of the most valuable ever sent out by the church.

Nine years ago she was called to give her youngest daughter to the service of the Lord as a Foreign Missionary of the American Board in Asia Minor. For a time it was a struggle, but grace triumphed and she gave her daughter unreservedly to this service. **Nor** did she ever repent having done so. Her efforts and her prayers were perhaps more earnest in this direction than in any other because of her intensified interest in the foreign work. No guest was ever more welcome to her hospitable home than a foreign missionary.

In her first letter to her daughter May, after sailing, written from Lake Mahopac she says:—

"I cannot tell you how badly I felt on Saturday, after I had said good-bye. Dear May, you have always been a great comfort to me. I thank the Lord for giving me so many dear children. I want to tell you what a sweet service we had on Sabbath. You may remember it was Communion. Mr. Schenck prayed for you both, asking that God would bring you safely to your destination, and bless you in your work as you had left father and mother and friends and had gone to carry the gospel to the perishing. And then he prayed for us, that we would be sustained and comforted. It seemed as if the dear Lord then and there came to me and quieted my heart."

In April, 1890, the twentieth annual meeting of the Woman's Board of Foreign Missions met in the First Presbyterian Church, Elmira, N. Y. Though very timid about public work, yet a sense of duty induced her to accept the position of a delegate. A correspondent of the *New York Observer*, a stranger to the family, in a report of the meeting, says:—

"Mrs. Peter Carter, of New York, at a consecration meeting, rose in her place among the delegates and with a voice full of tears urged the mothers present to let their daughters go as missionaries. She well knew whereof she spoke, her own daughter being a missionary in Turkey. It was such a sweet privilege to give one's children to the work of the Lord in heathen lands. The sacrifice would not be forgotten by the dear Lord, to whose service they were given, when it was lovingly and cheerfully done."

A pleasant incident occurred some years ago illustrating her interest in all missionaries. Mrs. Carter was one day crossing the ferry to New York, and observed sitting opposite to her a gentleman and lady with a number of little children and a great many bags and bundles. From the labels on the luggage she inferred they had been travelling from San Francisco. After watching them for some little time, she concluded with her remarkable discernment that they were missionaries returning from some foreign field. As the boat entered the slip she went across the cabin and spoke to the tired mother. It was as she supposed. They were homeward bound from China. Mrs. Carter asked the mother if she could not carry something for her to the dock where she expected to meet her father.

To her surprise and amusement, the baby was placed in her arms. Needless to say she carried the precious burden carefully ashore and stood with it in her arms till father and daughter had met and exchanged affectionate greetings.

In the Scotch church in New York some years ago, there was a cultivated Christian gentleman who had been born and brought up a Mohammedan. The reading of the New Testament put into his hands by a missionary was the means of his conversion. When he declared himself a Christian, his wife and children were taken from him. He was cast into prison and was subjected to great persecution. The missionaries found out his condition and procured his release with much difficulty. He came to America and became a member of the Scotch church. He was very poor and suffered for the want of many things. When Mrs. Carter heard of this, she started out one cold winter morning, and in a few hours collected sixty dollars for the relief of his immediate wants, and he never afterwards suffered for the want of anything.

Though so deeply interested in others

she never neglected her own. In the words of the wise man: "She looked well to the ways of her household and ate not the bread of idleness. Her children will rise up and call her blessed, her husband also and he praiseth her."

Her untiring devotion to her children is pleasantly illustrated in the following extract from one of her letters:—

"Yesterday morning I was going to do up pineapple preserves, when the bell rang and M^c (her son-in-law, Mr. Mann, then living in Bloomfield, N. J.) came in. I asked at once who was sick. He replied that Peter had tonsilitis. He had come up town to get some medicine, but that I need not go out as the child seemed better. However, there was the medicine Peter needed at once; downstairs were the pineapples; out in Bloomfield the sick child. Like the good grandmother you read about I said, 'I will go as soon as I can.' On the fire went the pineapples. In two hours I was through. I dressed in fifteen minutes, caught the 11.20 train, took a carriage and was soon at Fannie's. Peter was better but Fannie was so glad to see me."

It is most touching to recall that she took up the study of music again the last two years of her life for the sake of one of her boys. They took lessons and learned duets together, the mother practising quite as diligently as the son and with equal enjoyment.

Many of her summers were spent at Lake Mahopac where, in a roomy, old-fashioned mansion with a second story piazza overlooking the lake, she kept house for a dozen successive summers. Here troops of loving friends were entertained with that large-hearted hospitality which was so strikingly peculiar to her.

On one of these occasions, the company consisted of nine young men, who came on foot a distance of seventy miles, to spend a few days. They were cordially welcomed and lovingly entertained. Some of them were fine singers and for the time being, college songs were in the ascendant. Of course bathing and rowing were endless sources of entertainment.

She was exceedingly fond of her grandchildren, of whom she had six in Bloomfield, and they came often to see her. She always had a colored picture or a little pasteboard box or a wooden pill box for the little ones. And they never went away without an orange or a cracker. Grandma's crackers were somehow nicer than any others. Some of the grandchildren were very fond of music, and it was ever her delight to play and sing with them their favorite songs and hymns. One little grandson said a few days ago: "Mother, when I get to Heaven the first thing I will do, will be to ask for grandma's room."

The children and grandchildren at a distance were not forgotten by her. Every alternate month in the year, a box was sent to the daughter in Turkey. Her foresight and thoughtfulness were most remarkable, in supplying the wants in that far-away mission home. There were toys in almost every box for the little ones and at Christmas time the other missionaries of the station were remembered as well.

She wrote a regular weekly letter to her eldest daughter in Chicago. This she never omitted till her hand became too feeble to hold a pen.

Of late years she wrote a great many letters; delightfully bright and newsy letters they were.

Her hands were never idle. She was always knitting and sewing for her children or grandchildren. The last work she did was knitting an afghan for her eldest son.

No one can govern others until he has learned to govern himself. Mrs. Carter's servants were always deeply attached to her. Several of them staid with her for periods of eight or ten years. She seemed to have solved for herself the problem of domestic service. She was always thoughtful and considerate in dealing with them. She made it a rule never to speak when she was displeased about a matter, but waited until she had had time for quiet thought and prayer before giving reproof. Then she spoke calmly but firmly, and the effect was so different than it would have been had she spoken earlier. One housemaid became a devoted Christian while living with her. Another, who had been with her for eight years, sent her fruit while she was sick, and at the funeral, wept as she looked lovingly on the dear one who had been so long her friend. So beautiful was her faith, that she thought no matter too trivial to pray over. She never went to engage a new domestic but she laid the matter first before the Lord and asked his blessing upon it. No one in her employ ever left her in anger.

One special peculiarity of hers was a bright and happy temperament. Mr. A. D. F. Randolph, writing to her husband after her death, says:—

"It may have been months ago, and yet it seems only a very little while since I met her at the corner of the avenue. She seemed, as she always did, bright and cheery, as though the changes of years had brought no change to her. They had not, for the shadows of life were of the outside world merely, while within, the sun never set."

An old friend, Mr. Patrick Guthrie, of Edinburgh, writes: "I have never forgotten the very happy and delightful evening I spent in your house in 1882. I vividly recall the warmth and brightness of your dear wife's hospitality and kindness to me. 'To know her was to love her.'"

Another dear Edinburgh friend, Mr. Ferrier says: "I know that our gracious Lord will make the memory of her beautiful life an inspiration to you all. Her removal makes a most sensible blank when I think of our American friends and remember the bright and happy — I think I may say affectionate — welcome which I always received from her."

GATHERING SHADOWS.

"She is not lost, she is within the door
 That shuts out loss and every hurtful thing,
 With angels bright and loved ones gone before
 In her Redeemer's presence evermore
 And God himself her Lord and Judge and King."

SHE had long been conscious of heart trouble. It first manifested itself in the difficulty of going upstairs, which was one of the reasons for removing to the country. In the spring of 1892, the family removed to Bloomfield, N. J. Here she made many loving friends, and, while health and strength remained, rendered herself exceedingly useful in the ladies' societies of the First Presbyterian Church. One of the influential ladies of this church writes: "I cannot express the sadness I feel at the great loss that our Woman's Foreign Missionary Society has sustained in the death of Mrs. Carter. In fact every one who knew her feels that they have lost an earnest Christian friend and helper. She was such a power in our meetings. I feel as if a great prop had been removed from us."

In May, 1895, the heart trouble, with which she had been for some years more or less affected, manifested itself in new and aggravated forms such as at times in extreme shortness of breath, and at other times in a terrible sense of faintness caused, no doubt, by the irregular action of the heart. During the summer months, her days were spent on the piazza. Here her numerous friends called to see her. It was soon evident how greatly she was beloved. Though she had only been three years in Bloomfield, she could scarcely have had more loving or devoted friends had she always lived there.

One good woman said to a friend: "It is wonderful what a place Mrs. Carter has won in Bloomfield. Why you know Bloomfield people have the name of being very conservative. But they took Mrs. Carter for a leader in their benevolent society just as soon as they knew her.

And after she was confined to her room the ladies still leaned on her judgment, and kept coming to her for counsel and advice about their work."

She was very fond of flowers, and her friends, knowing this, kept her supplied with quantities of the most beautiful ones of all descriptions. She was able to ride three times a week, and this she greatly enjoyed. On Saturday afternoons, in company with her husband, these drives were sometimes extended to two hours or more.

Perhaps her greatest deprivation during the summer was her inability to attend church. Her pastor, Mr. Lee, was very attentive, and his visits and prayers were a great comfort to her. Speaking of one of these visits she said, " It was such a lovely prayer, and did me so much good."

Her husband and herself had been several times to Mohonk Lake, that sweet haven of rest for the tired children of God, and she was exceedingly anxious to see that lovely spot again. Some thought that she had not strength for the trip, but her physician rather favored it, and so on the 19th of September the journey was made. Everything that care could do was done to make the long ride in the train easy and comfortable. Her husband and a loving trained nurse accompanied her. She stood the journey much better than could have been anticipated, and the loving reception accorded to her by Mr. and Mrs. Smiley and their kind assistants was a great pleasure to her. Her husband's life-long friend, Rev. Dr. Cuyler, came a few days after, and this added much to her enjoyment. But the whole great household were her friends, and vied with each other in loving attentions.

Her patience in her sufferings was observed by all. One good woman said that this patience had been a blessed lesson to her and one that she would never forget.

She staid a fortnight at Mohonk and the homeward journey was borne with comparative comfort. The trip did her good. Her appetite was improved by it, and the pleasant people she met, especially two lady friends from the Scotch Church whom she had not seen for some time, cheered and interested her.

But from the day of her return she steadily declined. She could no longer lie down in bed, but spent her nights in a chair. The devoted nurse anticipated every want. Her eldest daughter from Chicago came home and spent the closing weeks with her, and with the other daughters watched over her night and day. Her eldest son also came frequently home from Princeton. So that all but the missionary daughter were much with her.

On Sabbath afternoon, Nov. 10, she seemed to be soundly sleeping, when all at once she said: "I hear every word you are saying." Her husband then repeated to her verses of hymns such as, "Jesus lover of my soul," "Just as I am without one plea," and the 23rd Psalm in the old

Scottish Metrical version, which was a great favorite of hers. These were followed by verses from scripture such as, "Let not your heart be troubled," "For God so loved the world," "This is a faithful saying," "The Spirit and the Bride say come," "Come unto me all ye that labor and are heavy laden" and so forth.

At frequent intervals she would say, "Go on," as if she were enjoying the sweet words. At the close she said, "Cannot we now have prayers?" So the little household all knelt in prayer together.

She seemed uncommonly bright, and knew every one present, and said some kind word of recognition to each.

Her husband said, "Do you know me, dear?"

"Certainly," she replied, adding with a smile and a good deal of vim, "I have known you for many a year."

One of her daughters said, "This is Douglas' birthday. He is twenty-one today."

She replied promptly, "Why so it is, and I have no birthday present for him, but he shall have one tomorrow."

A day or two after this, one of her daughters kneeling at her side said, "Mamma, Jesus is very precious to you. Is he not?"

"Yes indeed," she replied with emphasis, "He is very near, I cannot tell you how near." She stopped a moment and then added, "He said 'Come unto me' and I came."

Much of the time she seemed drowsy and unconscious of what was going on around her. At brief intervals she recognized the family till Saturday morning, November 16th at about 4 A. M., when a sudden change came, and without a struggle or a groan she went " to be with Christ."

In the language of another, "As she lay resting so sweetly with a look of perfect peace on her dear face, sleeping the blessed sleep that God gives his beloved, we could not think her dead. She had

only gone away. No, she did not die; she
only entered into life."

"In idle revery one winter's day,
I watched the narrow vista of a street,
Where crowds of men with noisy, hurrying feet
And eager eyes, went on their restless way.
Idly I noted where the boundary lay,
At which the distance did my vision cheat,
Past which each figure fading fast did fleet,
And seem to meet and vanish in the gray.
Sudden there came to me a thought oft told,
But newly shining then like flash of light,
This death the dread of which turns me so cold
Outside of our own fears has no stronghold;
'Tis but a boundary, past which in white,
Our friends are walking still, just out of sight."

HELEN HUNT JACKSON.

"I cannot and I will not say,
That she is dead, — she is just away.

With a cheery smile, and a wave of the hand,
She has wandered into an unknown land;

And left us dreaming how very fair
It needs must be, since she is there.

And you, O you, who the wildest yearn
For the old-time step and the glad return,

Think of her faring on, as dear
In the love of there as the love of here.

Think of her still as the same I say ;
She is not dead, she is just away."

LAST TRIBUTES.

Fold her, O Father, in thine arms,
And let her henceforth be
A messenger of love between
Our human hearts and Thee.
WHITTIER.

THE funeral services were held in her own home in Bloomfield, N. J., on Tuesday afternoon, November 19th, 1895, at 3 o'clock.

A large concourse of people from Bloomfield, Montclair, Glen Ridge, New York, Brooklyn and other places assembled to pay respect to the beloved one.

The services were participated in by her pastor, the Rev. James Beveridge Lee, Rev. T. L. Cuyler, D.D., of Brooklyn, Rev. George Alexander, D.D., of New York and the Rev. Alexander Dickson, D.D., of Lansingburgh, N. Y.

Comforting words from the Sacred Scriptures were read by Mr. Lee, and two of Mrs. Carter's favorite hymns, " My ain Countree" and " My Jesus as Thou wilt," were sung by Miss Eleanor McKee of New York, accompanied on the piano by her sister.

Mr. Lee said : —

The greater part of Mrs. Carter's Christian life was lived in the communion of the Scotch Presbyterian Church, New York. For three years she has been a regular worshipper and most faithful and helpful member of the First Presbyterian Church, of Bloomfield, (N. J.) Throughout life faithful to the purposes of the Christ, she is today inheriting His promises.

It may seem strange that, after only one year's acquaintance, even her pastor should attempt an estimate of her life. But my acquaintance was the last year and the best year of her life — the time when life's currents ran deepest, and life's outflow was broadest, the time when she was walking in the Land of Beulah, though neither she knew it nor we. In out-of-the-way places, during the past year, I have found growing, sometimes blossoming, the seeds of her kindnesses. In the public support of organizations for benevolent or missionary undertakings she was willing to lead or to take rank as she could best serve her Master, and whether leader or follower she gave stimulus and strength. The church at Rome, in Apostolic days, had in it such a helper. Paul speaks of her as one 'who labored much in the Lord.' He calls her 'The beloved Persis.' Mrs. Carter, who has labored much in the Lord, is our beloved Persis. The culture of her mind, the geniality of her disposition, the integrity of her character, the excellence of her judgment, the purity of her endeavor, the earnestness of her purpose and the largeness of her love — these are the qualities which endeared her to us all.

Pain and weariness seemed never able to blight the spirit with which she rejoiced in others' joys and sympathized in their sorrows. That many friends had learned from her Master the same lessons was evidenced by the many gifts, especially of flowers, which brightened her sick chamber. It reminds me of what John Bunyan has written of the experiences of Christiana, the wife of Christian, the pilgrim, while she sojourned in Beulah. 'In this place,' says Bunyan, 'the children of the town would go into the King's gardens and gather nosegays for the pilgrims and bring them to them with much affection. With these the pilgrims' chambers were perfumed while they stayed there, and with these were their bodies anointed to go over the river when their appointed time was come.'

Let me read to you more that Bunyan says, for long ago he pictured what has just now come to pass: 'Now, while they lay here and waited for the good hour, there was a noise in the town that there was a post come from the Celestial City with matter of great importance to one Christiana, the wife of Christian the pilgrim. So inquiry was made for her, and the house was found where she was, so the post presented her with a letter, the contents whereof were, 'Hail good woman, I bring thee tidings that the Master calleth for thee; and expecteth that thou shouldst stand in his presence in clothes of immortality within this ten days.' Now the day drew on that Christiana must be gone. So the road was full of people to see her take her journey. But, behold, all the banks beyond the river were full of horses and chariots, which were come down from above to accompany her to the city gate. So she came forth and entered the river with a beckon of farewell to those that followed her to the river-side. So her children and friends returned to their place, for that *those that waited for Christiana had carried her out of their sight.*'

"Were one touch lacking to complete Bunyan's picture, it might be finished with this: And a messenger of the King brought a letter sealed with the royal seal and addressed to the remaining pilgrims in

Beulah, that in the reading of it they might find comfort. And when they had broken the seal, the pilgrims read the writing and rejoiced much in its message. And the writing which was written was this : —

"*Whom He justified, them He also glorified.*"

Rev. Dr. Theodore L. Cuyler said : —

I am not here today in any official capacity, for I have never been the pastor of this dear household. My heart brings me here this afternoon, and the few simple words I shall utter come from my heart. We are bidden not only to "**rejoice with them that do rejoice,**" but "**weep with them that weep,**" and I have come today to grasp the hand, in this the hour of his great sorrow, of one of the most dearly beloved friends I have in all the world, none, in fact, more so than he outside of my own loved household. And I have known him before this sweet, sacred union was formed that has now been stricken asunder by God's own hand, ere long to be

Last Tributes. 51

formed again in the better world. I have known these two as husband and wife clear back to the time when they were made one in the Lord, nearly forty years ago.

A very bright, happy, beautiful life is that which has just passed from among us up into the higher life and glory of the Father's house. Mrs. Carter was happy in her parentage. Her father, as many of you know, was eminent as a Bible scholar, eminent as an office-bearer and a leader in the Church of Jesus Christ. Her mother was a Hannah, who lent her children to the Lord and found rich blessing. Very happy too, was Mrs. Carter in the union which God had formed; for I believe such unions are indeed made in Heaven. And all these years the sunshine has shone, and domestic love and peace have prevailed, and best of all the dear Master has been one of their household.

In choosing her path in life, she did not choose one that led her out into the public eye. Rather did she choose another style of service. She wrote no books, figured not much in a public capacity in the service of her Master. She knew well the deep, solemn, sacred, far-reaching duties that belong to the wife-hood and the Christian mother-hood. She had gauged rightly the dimensions of the Home that underlies church and commonwealth and the welfare of the Master's Kingdom. Therefore it was that she found her realm here, and her most sacred and sweetest life-duties were performed here. She looked well to the ways of her household; she reared up her children in the nurture and admonition of the Lord.

She found her empire here among her own family, an empire of love. And she chose wisely. It could be said of this Mary as was said by the Master of another in olden days: " Mary has chosen the good part that shall never be taken from her," and she found her rich and blessed reward in all the joys that a hallowed and holy home life brings, joys in a life never marred for one moment by him who made her a part of his very self. Great reward reaped she as a parent in rearing up a group of sons and daughters of whom any parent in this world might well be proud.

And now it seems to me that this is not a complete bereavement. She still lives — lives in these beloved children, born of her, trained by her, consecrated by her to the Master, bearing her blood and to a great degree her image. She lives in them, through them and by them so that when my dear brother looks on them day by day, and receives night after night the good-night kiss, he will feel as if somehow it was the mother's face and the mother's lips that were speaking and embracing. Thank God for faithful mothers!

And in another sense, still more sublime, she lives. Never more than at this very hour. To be sure the form slumbers, concealed in the casket among this company that gathers around. To be sure the lips that spoke hospitable welcome to us so often are silent. To be sure the busy hands, busy in all services of wifely and motherly love, repose at her side unmoving, but the everlasting life begun at the cross of Christ has simply passed over by the wonderful transition which we cannot fathom, from this world into the better; for there is perfect continuity, bear in mind, between the life begun here *in* Christ and the life perfected *with* Christ. For here there are certain imperfections and certain incompletenesses, and it must be so, but from the very hour that the mortal is put off and the immortal is put on, from the very hour that the atmosphere of this world, with whatever it has of trouble, has been left behind, and the soul, redeemed, passes into the glorious atmosphere of Heaven, then life comes in its indescribable abundance, its exceeding weight of glory. And now into that life in its completeness and its fulness our dear friend and sister in the Lord Jesus Christ has passed within the last few hours.

It was a slow, steady transition. For many months it has been gradually drawing nearer to the end. Christiana surrounded by her children, moving on toward the Celestial City, happy in their love, watched over, tenderly cared for, she passed along through the Beulah Land of her pilgrimage. Without any fear, without any doubt, in the sunshine of the Master, surrounded by everything that love can bestow, she came at last to the unbridged river, and the waves were parted before her steps, and she has gone in to that Home, of which, if we could see what she has already seen, we would wish ourselves among them.

Now that she has passed into this blessed life everlasting, into the joy and glory of her Master's presence, there is only left behind her silent, slumbering form. What the Apostle calls the "tent" which the spirit casts off when it ascends into the presence of the Glorious King on high. And ere long you will take up this form, and gently and lovingly bear her away from the home she loved to that silent spot, just such a spot as her Master, and your and my Master, rested in, that he might conquer the grave and become the first-fruits of all that sleep. So has God given His beloved sleep, and today we may all say : —

"Sleep on, beloved, now and take thy rest;
Lay down thy head upon thy Saviour's breast;
We loved thee well, but Jesus loves thee best;
    Good-night! Good-night!

" Calm is thy slumber as an infant's sleep;
But thou shalt wake no more to toil and weep:
Thine is a perfect rest, secure and deep;
    Good-night! Good-night!

" Until made beautiful by Love Divine,
Thou, in the likeness of thy Lord shalt shine,
And He shall bring that golden crown of thine,
    Good-night! Good-night!

"Only 'Good-night,' beloved, not 'farewell!'
A little while, and all His saints shall dwell
In hallowed union indivisible,
    Good-night! Good-night!

"Until we meet again before His throne,
Clothed in the spotless robe He gives His own,
Until we know even as we are known,
  Good-night! Good-night!"

Dr. George Alexander said: —

It would better accord with the feelings of my heart to take my place with those who sit in silence, communing with their own thoughts, meditating on their great loss, and suffering the tide of grateful and sorrowful emotion to surge over them.

I first knew our dear friend as a bride. In those dear old days, I was led, a barefoot boy, to see and admire the young wife of my mother's dearest friend. In later years it has been my frequent privilege to be admitted to the household over which she presided. Love for that household, and sympathy for them in their unmeasured loss has brought me here to-day.

It has not been my lot to see her while walking through that Beulah land, where the shining ones come forth to meet the pilgrims toward the Celestial City. In my memory she must ever be, not the patient sufferer, blessing the chastening hand of her Heavenly Father, but the very embodiment of health and gladness. I think of her first and chiefly as the Christian homemaker, investing her home with the joy and the heavenly charm which should ever be the heritage of the godly, the familiar friend of her children, and the one in whom the heart of her husband did safely trust.

How wide-reaching has been her influence! With what beauty and grace she filled her station, and did her work! Her children, to whom she made the way of godliness supremely attractive, rise up today and call her blessed. Whether mingling their tears in this presence, or, in the far East, exposed to the perils of Moslem fanaticism, they hold in their hearts, along with the image of their Saviour, the image of a mother who is now rejoicing in the beatific vision, and find a new and precious meaning in those familiar words of comfort, "In my Father's house are many mansions. . . . . I go to prepare a place for you."

The Prayer by Dr. Dickson.

Our Father who art in Heaven : If we had six wings like the Seraphim, with twain we would cover our face, with twain we would cover our feet, and with twain we would fly into Thy bosom, for Thou art our refuge and strength, a very present help in trouble. But we have no wings, as yet, and we cannot fly. We cannot even come to Thee except Thou shalt draw us. Draw us now to Thyself by the cords of Thy best love and by this great bereavement. Draw us nearer to Thy side than we have ever been before, and let us lie down, in love's own place on Thy breast, so that we shall feel Thy gentle heart beating responsive to our own, and Thou shalt hear the breathing of our desires, which neither speech nor language can express. In the heart of our hearts sorrow and joy are striving together for the mastery. Let it please Thee, while we are yet speaking, to grant us so much of Thy sweet mercy and grace, that the sorrow shall fly away and only joy be left; and in the multitude of our thoughts within us may Thy comforts delight our souls.

Hear our prayer, O Lord, and give ear unto our cry; hold not Thy peace at our tears; for we are strangers with Thee and sojourners, as all our fathers were. Passing through this wilderness, to the better country, we have come to our Marah, and the waters are so bitter that we cannot drink them. In answer to our earnest and united request show us the tree, which when cast into the waters, the waters shall be made sweet. We are come to our juniper bush, and like Thy servant of old time we are prostrated with overmuch sorrow, and greatly discouraged because of the way. Hear Thou the voice of our affliction and speak to the angel who knows the way hither; command him to make haste, and fly away swiftly to us, bringing with him a cruse of water, fresh dipped from the river, clear as crystal, for us, and with his shining hand to kindle another fire of coals and bake another cake for us, and then to touch us once and again, saying, "Arise and eat, because the journey is too great for thee:" and in the strength of Thy timely repast may we rise up and go on our way, sorrowful yet always rejoicing, till we reach the mount of God in heaven.

Almighty and most merciful Father; we remember all the way which Thou hast led us these forty years, and this is the most dreadful place; this is our Gethsemane; and this is our Gethsemane prayer, O our Father, if this cup may not pass away from us, except we drink it, Thy will be done. Send down to us the Gethsemane angel, who ministered strength and comfort to Thy dear Son, our Saviour, that he may help us also, saying, "This is the cup thy

Father hath given thee to drink; drink more of it; drink all of it." Blessed be thy name though the cup be bitter, it is not bottomless, and as we lift it to our quivering lips by the transforming power of Thy love, let it be changed into a cup of blessing.

Dear Lord Jesus, we must come to Thee thyself for Thou art the **brother born for adversity**; our own best brother, whom bereavement brings to better view; a substitute for all when all is gone; all without all, as well as all in all. Whom have we in Heaven but Thee, and there is none upon earth that we desire besides thee. Oh, magnify Thy merciful kindness to us and make this hour of darkness the beginning of the beatific vision. As the Son of God Thou art able to do for us exceeding abundantly above all that we ask or think, and as the Son of Man and a man of sorrows Thou canst sympathize with us in all our afflictions. Let it please Thee to have pity upon us and save us out of all our troubles. We rejoice to know that when hanging on the cross for us Thy last thoughts were concerning Thy mother, and Thy last words were addressed to Thy mother, providing a son and a home for her when the sword was piercing through her soul; and knowing the strength and sweetness of a mother's love, and knowing how hard it is to part with one so near and dear, let Thy divine and human compassion be lavished on these motherless children. Behold, and bless them every one. Remember the first-born who, following her loving heart, left her husband and children to take care of themselves, and came home that she might be an angel of blessing to her mother during her last days, when she was watching and praying and patiently waiting for the love-paved chariot to come and take her away out of all tribulation. May the same benediction abide with her sisters who are here present and with all their children; cover them with Thy feathers, comfort them with Thy love, and may they always have the good-will of Him that dwelt in the bush. Bless these brothers who are bowed down, heavily mourning for their mother; bring them into the secret of Thy presence, and keep them there. Lay both Thy hands upon their heads and so bless them that they shall be a blessing. We cannot forget the youngest sister, who, when she went to the heathen, took all her heart away with her, and left it all at home. In the arms of our faith and love we would lift her up out of the darkness into the brightest light of Thy smiling face. Speak one word to her; say unto her, "Mary," and may she be able to respond right heartily, saying, "Rabboni, which is to say Master," which is to say *my* master. Hold her in the hollow of Thy hand; keep her as the apple of Thine eye; hide her under the shadow of Thy wings. O Thou who savest by Thy right hand them which put their trust in Thee from those that rise up against them, show Thy marvellous loving-kindness to thine own dear Mary, and all the precious members of her family. Awake, why sleepest Thou, O Lord ? Why withdrawest Thou Thy hand, even Thy right hand? Pluck it out of Thy bosom for their defence. And when they have done serving Thee for love of Thee, bring them to Thine everlasting kingdom.

Dearest Lord Jesus, in our message to Thy mercy seat the last shall be first. Look down in tenderest love and pity upon Thy servant whose heart is in the casket here with his beloved; and who is left so lonely and desolate and sad. We praise Thee that he had such a loving wife so long, that he was not called to part with her till he was drawing so near the lifted gates of the Lamb-lit city, that the light thereof came shining through them to beautify his gray hairs which are a crown of glory because they are found in the way of righteousness. Permit him to lean on the arm of Thine almightiness till the twain shall be one again in the home that shall never be left desolate, and where death-divided friends shall meet to part no more.

In the greatness of our grief we give Thee glory in the highest for the life of thine handmaid. We thank Thee that she was such a beautiful Christian, adorning the doctrine of God, her Saviour, in all things. We bless Thee that she was more and better than a good Samaritan in this community, as she went about through these highways and byways pouring the oil and wine of love human and divine into hearts wounded by sin and sorrow. Especially would we magnify Thy name, that having loved Thee all her life with all her heart, and having served Thee all her life for love, she is still loving and serving Thee in love's own country, where the inhabitant shall not say, I am sick; neither can they die any more, for they are equal unto the angels.

We cannot forget to thank, Thee, O Lord our Lord, for what this mother in Israel was to us; for the heart she carried in her hand to us; for the sweet smile and the holy kiss with which she always greeted us; and the loving hospitality with which she entertained us. Glory be to the Father, when we were strangers she took us in, and made us members of her family.

Jesus Master, be not angry with us, and we will make one more request. We do not know what holy service this mother may have in Heaven, but if she may be excused, and if it may please Thee, send her down to be the guardian angel of her missionary daughter, who is in perils by the heathen. And though a thousand may fall at her side, and ten thousand at her right hand, let no evil come nigh her. And, when a few more bitter cups and cups of blessing have been given her to drink, may she be caught up to Paradise to learn more of Thy love from Thine own lips which are like lilies dropping sweet smelling myrrh. And unto the King eternal, immortal, invisible, the only wise God, and our own God, and our exceeding joy shall be all the glory, world without end. *Amen.*

AT THE PARTING.

SELECTIONS REPEATED TO THE FAMILY BY DR. DICKSON.

Consider the lilies of the field how they grow; they toil not, neither do they spin; and yet I say unto you, That even Solomon in all his glory was not arrayed like one of these. I am the Rose of Sharon, and the lily of the valleys. As the lily among thorns, so is my love among the daughters. My beloved is gone down into his garden, to the beds of spices, to feed in the gardens, and to gather lilies.

Hearken, O daughter, and consider, and incline thine ear; forget also thine own people, and thy father's house; so shall the King greatly desire thy beauty; for He is thy Lord; and worship thou Him. The King's daughter is all glorious within; her clothing is of wrought gold. She shall be brought unto the King in raiment of needlework; the virgins her companions that follow her shall be brought unto thee. With gladness and rejoicing shall they be brought; they shall enter into the King's palace.

I heard as it were the voice of a great multitude, and as the voice of many waters and as the voice of mighty thunderings, saying, Alleluia; for the Lord God omnipotent reigneth. Let us be glad and rejoice, and give honour to Him; for the marriage of the Lamb is come, and His wife hath made herself ready. And to her it was granted that she should be arrayed in fine linen, clean and white: for the fine linen is the righteousness of saints. And He saith unto me, write, Blessed are they which are called unto the marriage supper of the Lamb.

The voice of my Beloved! behold He cometh leaping upon the mountains, skipping upon the hills. My Beloved is like a roe, or a young hart; behold He standeth behind our wall, He looketh forth at the windows, showing Himself through the lattice. My Beloved spake, and said unto me, Rise up, my love, my fair one, and come away. For lo, the winter is past, the rain is over and gone; the flowers appear on the earth; the time of the singing of birds is come, and the voice of the turtle is heard in our land; the fig-tree putteth forth her green figs, and the vines with the tender grape give a good smell. Arise, my love, my fair one, and come away.

I am now ready to be offered, and the time of my departure is at hand. I am in a strait betwixt two, having a desire to depart and to be with Christ which is far better. Lord, now lettest thou Thy servant depart in peace, according to Thy word for mine eyes have seen Thy salvation. For to me to live is Christ and to die is gain.

The word of the Lord came unto me, saying, Son of man, behold, I take away from thee the desire of thine eyes with a stroke; yet neither shalt thou mourn nor weep, neither shall thy tears run down. Forbear to cry, make no mourning for the dead. For so He giveth His beloved sleep. But I would not have you to be ignorant, brethren, concerning them which are asleep, that ye sorrow not, even as others which have no hope. For if we believe that Jesus died and rose again, even so them also which sleep in Jesus will God bring with Him. For this we say unto you by the word of the Lord, that we which are alive and remain unto the coming of the Lord shall not prevent them which are asleep. For the Lord himself shall descend from heaven with a shout, with the voice of the archangel, and with the trump of God; and the dead in Christ shall rise first; then we which are alive and remain shall be caught up together with them in the clouds, to meet the Lord in the air; and so shall we ever be with the Lord. Wherefore, comfort one another with these words.

The Lord gave, and the Lord hath taken away; blessed be the name of the the Lord. Trust ye in the Lord **forever**; for in the Lord Jehovah **is** everlasting strength. The eternal God **is** thy refuge, and underneath are the **everlasting arms.** Now, the God of hope fill you with all joy and peace in believing, that ye may abound in hope, through the power of the Holy Ghost.

AFTER THE PARTING.

SELECTIONS REPEATED BY DR. DICKSON.

Who shall separate us from the love of Christ? Shall tribulation, or distress, or persecution, or famine, or nakedness, or peril, or sword? As it is written, For thy sake we are killed all the day long; we are accounted as sheep for the slaughter. Nay in all these things we are more than conquerors, through Him that loved us. For I am persuaded, that neither death nor life, nor angels, nor principalities, nor powers, nor things present, nor things to come, nor height, nor depth, nor any other creature, shall be able to separate us from the love of God which is in Christ Jesus our Lord.

I know, O Lord, that Thy judgements are right, and that Thou in faithfulness hast afflicted me. I know that my Redeemer liveth, and that He shall stand at the latter day upon the earth; and though after my skin worms destroy this body, yet in my flesh shall I see God; whom I shall see for myself, and mine eyes shall behold, and not another. We know that if our earthly house of this tabernacle were dissolved, we have a building of God, an house not made with hands, eternal in the

Heavens. We know that all things work together for good, to them that love God, to them that are called according to His purpose. Beloved, now are we the sons of God, and it doth not yet appear what we shall be; but we know that, when He shall appear, we shall be like Him; for we shall see Him as He is.

I heard a voice from Heaven saying unto me, Write, Blessed are the dead which die in the Lord from henceforth: Yea, saith the Spirit, that they may rest from their labours; and their works do follow them. Blessed are they that do his commandments, that they may have right to the tree of life, and may enter in through the gates into the city. Blessed are the pure in heart; for they shall see God. They shall see His face; and His name shall be in their foreheads. Blessed are they that mourn; for they shall be comforted.

The Lord is my shepherd; I shall not want. He maketh me to lie down in green pastures; He leadeth me beside the still waters. He restoreth my soul; He leadeth me in the paths of righteousness for His name's sake. Yea, though I walk through the valley of the shadow of death, I will fear no evil; for thou art with me; Thy rod and Thy staff they comfort me. Thou preparest a table before me in the presence of mine enemies; Thou anointest my head with oil; my cup runneth over. Surely goodness and mercy shall follow me all the days of my life; and I will dwell in the house of the Lord forever.

I will lift up mine eyes unto the hills, from whence cometh my help. My help cometh from the Lord, which made Heaven and earth. He will not suffer thy foot to be moved; He that keepeth thee will not slumber. Behold, He that keepeth Israel shall neither slumber nor sleep. The Lord is thy keeper; The Lord is thy shade upon thy right hand. The sun shall not smite thee by day, nor the moon by night. The Lord shall preserve thee from all evil; He shall preserve thy soul. The Lord shall preserve thy going out and thy coming in from this time forth, and even for evermore.

It was now dark, and Jesus was not come to them. And the sea arose by reason of a great wind that blew. The ship was now in the midst of the sea, tossed with waves; for the wind was contrary. And in the fourth watch of the night Jesus went unto them, walking on the sea. And immediately He talked with them, and saith unto them, Be of good cheer; it is I; be not afraid. Then they willingly received Him into the ship; and immediately they were at the land whither they went.

When the great storm came it was night; and the night was dark; and the disciples were in the midst of the sea; about three miles from either shore; and the wind was contrary, and should have driven them back to the land whence they sailed; but strange to say it carried them quickly into the port whither they were bound. Immediately they were at the land whither they went. So He bringeth them unto their desired haven. So He bringeth us unto our desired haven. Arise, let us go hence.

The interment took place on Wednesday, November 20th. Many followed the dear body to its last resting place in Woodlawn Cemetery, where it was lovingly laid beside those of her three little children, her father, mother and sisters, till the Lord comes again; when " the dead in Christ shall rise first."

The following words were said by the Rev. Dr. Dickson at the grave: —

That which thou sowest is not quickened except it die. It is sown a natural body, it is raised a spiritual body. Except a corn of wheat fall into the ground and die, it abideth alone; but if it die it bringeth forth much fruit. It is sown in dishonour, it is raised in glory. And as we have borne the image of the earthy, we shall also bear the image of the heavenly.

   Unveil thy bosom, faithful tomb!
      Take this new treasure to thy trust;
   And give these sacred relics room
      To seek a slumber in the dust.

   Nor pain, nor grief, nor anxious fear,
      Invade thy bounds: no mortal woes
   Can reach the lovely sleeper here,
      And angels watch her soft repose.

   So Jesus slept: God's dying son
      Passed through the grave and blessed the bed.
   Rest here, fair saint, till from His throne
      The morning break, and pierce the shade.

   Break from His throne, illustrious morn!
      Attend, O earth, His sovereign word!
   Restore thy trust, O glorious form!
      She must ascend to meet her Lord.

My Beloved is mine, and I am His; He feedeth among the lilies. Behold thou art fair my Beloved, yea, pleasant; also our bed is green. His left hand is under my head, and His right hand doth embrace me; For so He giveth His beloved sleep.

Jesus said unto her, I am the resurrection, and the life; he that believeth in me, though he were dead, yet shall he live; and whosoever liveth, and believeth in me shall never die. Jesus saith unto her, Mary. She turned herself, and saith unto Him, Rabboni, which is to say Master.

Mary, the Lord bless thee and keep thee. The Lord make His face to shine upon thee, and be gracious unto thee. The Lord lift up His countenance upon thee, and give thee peace.

Dearest sister, sweetest lover, divinest mother, thou hast been our morning angel, our midday angel, and our midnight angel, making our home more like Heaven, by thy sweet presence here, henceforth thou shalt make our Heaven more like home, by thy sweet presence there. Patiently, prayerfully, hopefully thou hast passed through all thy toilsome days and wearisome nights, now rest in peace, and may thy rest be glorious. We praise God for thee, and for thy lovely lamb-like life; and we hope to praise God with thee, when Jesus comes; till then farewell.

Let us Pray.

Jesus Master, who was dead and is alive for evermore, we commit to Thee Thyself this body, which was made by Thee, and redeemed by Thee, and is still united to Thee. Come Thou to Thy consecrated parcel of ground, and with the keys hanging at thy girdle, lock this precious treasure in this place of peaceful rest; and let Thine eyes and Thine heart be over this temple of the Holy Ghost, till it shall be built again. Before we depart hence, and while we are yet speaking, according to thy promise, hear our prayer, and send hither all the angels of the sepulcher —

the twain that sat as sentinels, one at Thy head and the other at Thy feet, when Thou wast sleeping in the grave for us. Send also the angel who rolled away the stone for Thee; and Michael, the archangel, who contended for the body of Moses; that together they may watch, and guard, and keep and if need be defend this blood-bought, blood-washed body of Thy bride, till Thou shalt come again and she shall live again in the likeness of Thine own glorious body. And in that day when she shall put off these ashen robes and put on the wedding garment, and rise to the marriage mansion and the marriage supper, let there be no strife between these ministering spirits, which of them shall have the honour and the pleasure of presenting her at the Court of Heaven, where she shall see the King in His beauty, and be crowned by Him the Queen in gold of Ophir. And to Thy dear name, dearest, sweetest, kindest Lord shall be all the glory, world without end. *Amen.*

It never can be wrong to do as Jesus did, and as He sometimes called His friends by name, I will follow His example in closing these sacred services.

Nannie: Wait on the Lord; be of good courage, and He shall strengthen thine heart; wait I say on the Lord. For the Lord thy God, He it is that doth go with thee, He will not fail thee nor forsake thee.

Fannie: Fear thou not; for I am with thee; be not dismayed; for I am thy God; I will strengthen thee: yea, I will help thee; yea I will uphold thee with the right hand of my righteousness. I will never leave thee nor forsake thee.

Nellie: I know thee by name, and thou hast also found grace in my sight. The mountains shall depart and the hills be removed; but my kindness shall not depart from thee, neither shall the covenant of my peace be removed, saith the Lord that hath mercy on thee. Behold, I have graven thee upon the palms of my hands.

Jesse: My son, hear the instruction of

thy father, and forsake not the law of thy mother; for they shall be an ornament of grace unto thy head and chains about thy neck. When thou goest, it shall lead thee; when thou sleepest, it shall keep thee; and when thou awakest, it shall talk with thee.

Douglas: He that loveth father or mother more than me is not worthy of me. I will not leave you comfortless; I will come to you. As one whom his mother comforteth so will I comfort you and ye shall be comforted. Cast thy burden upon the Lord, and He shall sustain thee.

There remaineth yet the youngest daughter; her mother's namesake, so far away and yet so near and dear. Jesus saith unto her, Mary: I have called thee by thy name, thou art mine. Thou shalt not be afraid for the terror by night; nor for the arrow that flieth by day. Because thou hast made the Lord which is my refuge, even the Most High thy habitation, there shall no evil befall thee, neither shall any plague come nigh thy dwelling. For He shall give His angels charge over thee, to keep thee in all thy ways.

My beloved brother Peter: Let not your heart be troubled: ye believe in God, believe also in me. In my Father's house are many mansions; if it were not so, I would have told you. I go to prepare a place for you. And if I go and prepare a place for you, I will come again and receive you unto myself; that where I am there ye may be also. Peace I leave with you, my peace I give unto you. Let not your heart be troubled, neither let it be afraid.

The Benediction.

REMINISCENCES.

"*We shall miss thee at a thousand turns, along life's
    weary track,
Not a sorrow or a joy, but we shall long to call thee back,
Yearn for thy true and gentle heart, long thy bright smile
    to see,
For many dear and true are left, but none are quite like
    thee.*"

THE youngest daughter, Mary Carter Dodd, now a missionary of the American Board in Turkey, writes thus: —

It is such a pleasure for me to give some of my memories of my precious mother. I love to live over again in thought the good old days when we were boys and girls together living in our father's house.

To begin with, let me quote the words of my Armenian nurse girl who has been with me eight years, and who went with me to America in 1890. When she heard what I was doing she said, "Write love ilay doloo idi," (she was full of love.) She was certainly a very loving mother, ready to do anything for her children, planning and caring for them in her thoughtful way.

It seems to me that I have special reason to realize this, for though she could not run in and help me as she could my sisters, yet she was always planning and thinking of my comfort. The boxes that have come so regularly every two months since we left home, and which have been such a source of delight to us all, were always filled with evidences of her love. It was really wonderful to me how she could know so well just what I needed. It almost seemed as if she could read my thoughts. A month ago, when I was laid aside for a few days with influenza, I wanted some soft, warm slippers for my feet. Rummaging in the boxes, I came across a neat pair of gray worsted slippers. Drawing them on, I noticed there was a piece of paper in one, and opening it, I found written on it "from mother." That was only one of many tokens of her thoughtful, constant love.

Was there ever such a neat little body as our mother? From the crown of her head to the tips of her toes she was tidy and trim. As for her house, in what good order it was kept. We girls can remember with feelings almost of awe, her beautiful dainty bed, with its spotless cover. No one ever made it but herself, and we would watch her as she smoothed out, patted down and pulled things into shape. We never dared lay anything on its immaculate spread and to play on it, or even to lie on it, would have been considered sacrilege.

What great care she took of the old mahogany furniture that had been handed down for several generations. As I remember it, it never showed signs of wear though in constant use.

As I go about my household cares, I often think how mother would do this and that piece of work. How many times I have longed to have her come in and inspect my house-keeping, pointing out to me my faults and telling me how I might correct them. But since I have never had that privilege, I can only try to do what she taught me to when I was a girl.

When we came home from school, when we were children, our first question was, "Is mamma home?" and she was generally looking out for us. But if she had to be away, I remember how empty the house seemed to us.

We cannot any of us forget her fondness for her flowers. They would blossom when those in other people's windows only showed leaves. They knew she loved them, and responded to her tender touch. The flowers in the windows gave a touch of brightness to the otherwise sombre brown stone house.

One of the happiest times of the day to us children was the evening hour when we were waiting for father to come home to dinner. Mother would light the front parlor chandeliers and sit down to the piano to play, and her lively music would quickly bring us around her. Favorite airs were called for, and if she sang there was always a hearty chorus from us children. If any of us were drearily studying upstairs, when we heard the stirring notes, down would go books and papers and away we flew to join in the music. We did so love to hear her play! She played with so much enthusiasm and enjoyment that it seemed as if her playing must be better than other people's. How I love to read over the Scottish ballads she was so fond of singing. I can almost hear her voice as I read, and the songs now seem sacred to me so entirely are they associated with her.

Our Sunday evening singing hour was always so enjoyable. It is one of the pleasantest memories I have of the dear old home in 28th street. We all chose hymns that we liked, mother usually playing, but as we grew older, we were allowed to try our hand, and when mistakes were made every one was patient and not overcritical. Mother enjoyed it as much as any of us.

Our next door neighbors used to say they always knew when we were at dinner. One evening we had been unusually jolly when mother turning around to a dear friend of the family, who was visiting us, said, " Doesn't this noise make you crazy Dr. ——?" When the unexpected reply " Yes ma'am," came, mother was somewhat chagrined and nonplussed. But the next minute she was reassured when her guest, who dearly loved a joke, burst into a hearty laugh.

Her birthday was in August, and we usually made quite a celebration of it. One year she went away on a visit the day before and did not return till the evening of her birthday, so that the day was not specially marked. Happening to discover the next day that she had missed the usual little celebration, we determined to give her a surprise. Accordingly the following afternoon we trimmed the dining room with flowers, making a bower of greens at mother's place at the table and in the bower, over the chair was hung a placard inscribed "In honor of the second day after the anniversary of the birthday of our mother," and every article of food at the table was labeled in the same way. After the blinds were tightly closed and the numerous Japanese lanterns hanging about the room were lighted we brought mother in and she was greatly surprised and very grateful in spite of the extreme heat of the shut-up room and the rather prickly nature of her bower.

We always loved to have mother go away visiting or see any sights for when she came home she had so much to tell. She had such sharp eyes she saw everything that went on around her, nothing escaped her and she would relate it all in such a graphic, breezy way. There was only one draw-back to her visiting in our childish eyes. She would always bring back such glowing accounts of the behavior of the small girls and boys where she visited and hold them up to us as such bright examples that we fairly loathed them and were ready to declare that we could not let her go away again.

I can never forget the trouble she took in shopping with me before my wedding. How many hours she spent with me tramping from store to store. No trouble was too great for her. She even marked with her own hand, all my table linen, bed-linen and underclothing, no small item of itself. Now I constantly come across her writing on my household things.

The last time I was home, when my little baby, Nellie, was so ill, I never can cease from being grateful to her for all the care she took of her. She seemed to feel a personal responsibility for her, and worked over her constantly. How relieved she was when she began to improve.

Her sister, Mrs. Knapp, writes the following: —

Among my first recollections of Mary was her wedding day and seeing her husband and herself receive the congratulations of their friends. She was the first daughter to leave home, and accordingly her little romance made a deep impression on the minds of her little sisters.

When the new home was set up and the furnishing began, it was all so interesting. The book-case in the parlor contained the "Arabian Nights' Entertainments," and this made Mary's house very attractive to me. I spent all my Saturday afternoons there reading.

It was at her house that I learned to eat oatmeal, and in the library to make the acquaintance of Burns and Scott. So the lives just united were beginning to influence others in a quiet way.

The years went by and I grew up to be a woman. I saw more and more each year what it was that made Mary's home so attractive. It was her wonderful unselfishness. Her hospitality was unbounded. With a large family of children to provide for, and so much sewing to do, it seemed as if company would be such an undertaking. But she was so unselfish, that she was willing to take all the trouble for the sake of the pleasure it would give others.

Everything went on in the most orderly manner with a houseful of guests. This broadened her own life, and awakened her sympathy in many other lives. Mrs. Henry Ward Beecher says :—

"A woman can do her own work, be her own dressmaker, and incidentally bring up a family of children, accomplishing all in a satisfactory manner, if she be upheld by the thought, that her husband's love and trust are placed upon her."

While Mary did not have to do all contained in the above quotation, she did bring up a large family of sons and daughters, providing for their many wants by economy and excellent management. Her husband's affection, pride and encouragement in her capability more than repaid her for the trouble she took, planning and working for them all.

It always seemed to me a lovely household, the heads of it being uniformly of one mind. As Longfellow says in "Hiawatha,"

> "As unto the bow, the cord is,
> So unto the man is woman,
> Though she bends him, she obeys him,
> Though she draws him yet she follows,
> Useless each without the other."

During the last few years, Mary and I grew very close to one another, and we had many confidential chats, about our homes and our children. She had lofty aspirations for her children, but always unworldly ones. Their spiritual good was nearest her heart.

It was not only for her family and kinsfolk she wrought, but for the poor and needy everywhere. She went out of her way to do helpful things for women in trouble. She climbed flights of tenement stairs, to give, by her cheerful presence, encouragement and hope to sorrow-stricken souls.

Much has gone out of my life, by the death of my unselfish sister Mary. But her memory will ever be bright in my home, and her influence for good undying.

Her niece, Mrs. I. W. Cochran writes:

Do you remember the day when you introduced me to Aunt Minnie on Fifth Avenue near 19th Street and I saw her for the first time. Afterwards you told me she was to be my aunt, and I was to call her Aunt Minnie because I had so many Aunt Marys.

Then came the wedding, an event of great interest to all of us children. How we all enjoyed going up to your dear little house in 26th Street.

It seems to me the most striking thing about Aunt Minnie was her motherhood. She was an ideal mother. Nothing better could be said of any woman. I never saw a more lovely and interesting group than those four little girls, so bright and healthy and natural, so loving and obedient, so merry and happy. She was merry and happy with them and not very much older. I remember once going into the 26th Street house nursery and she was telling me what a merry game they had been having together and how she said, "Oh dear, I feel as if I should go out of my head." And Nannie exclaimed, "Oh Mamma, how funny you would look!"

Her babies always went to sleep when she wanted them to, and woke up when she wanted them to, and were fed at regular times and consequently never had colic.

She was the best manager I ever saw. Her house, neat as a pin, her table liberal and elegant and such a pair of hands to turn off work. Her dress was always neat and tasteful. She told me once that she could go out in the worst of walking and come back with an immaculate white skirt.

As to the bringing up of her children,

there never was any forcing process. It was not a hothouse but a nursery. The young plants were trained away from what was hurtful and debasing up into God's pure air and sunshine. They soon learned to find pleasure in good books, and none of them had to be urged to study. It was in the home atmosphere and they took to it like ducks to water.

They were taught so naturally and simply, that the right way seemed to them the pleasant way. God was their friend and they never knew the time when they did not love Him.

You remember better than I do, the time when you both had the fruits of your united efforts, when all the four little girls came in one day saying that they wanted to be Christians. Dear little May was left out from the Communion table because she was so young, just as David was left out from Jesse's feast, but she was chosen of God for all that. But it was only for a little while she was left out, as the following year, May took her place with the others at the table of the Lord.

She never thought her children a trouble and never said they were too near of an age.

Another thing I remember about her was her willingness to oblige with her music. She said that her father had given her the best of advantages, vocal and instrumental, on condition that she would always play or sing when asked, not waiting to be urged. Though an accomplished musician and trained to sing very difficult music, when she found her husband liked Scotch ballads best, she learned them for his sake. She had her reward, for her beautiful rendering of these simple and heart-touching songs won her more admiration than her Italian Opera songs would have done. It was a line all her own. Then during the war she sang patriotic songs that pleased everybody.

My son told me since her death that when she was entertaining a houseful of young people last Christmas-tide she sang the dear old Scotch song, "I loe nae laddie but ane." She changed the name of Jamie in the last line and exclaimed "And now I am Peter's for life." Then she jumped up from the piano-stool and ran over and kissed you, blushing like a girl.

I always loved to get her letters. She wrote such a graceful little note in such a dainty way and always with some sweet thought in it.

Much as she loved May, I do not think she even for a moment grudged her to her Master, whom she loved better still. How greatly May's consecration increased her interest in missions! Where her treasure was there was her heart also. She seemed to have no worldly ambitions for her children, but was more than satisfied if they were serving God faithfully.

But above everything else I remember the love and sympathy she showed me in my own sorrows and especially about dear little Kitty. She came up to 53rd Street and spent the morning that Kitty died with us and sang Kitty's favorite hymns. She had a loving heart which was readily touched with the grief of others.

Her nephew, Rev. S. T. Carter, writes:

My earliest recollections are connected with my Uncle Peter. He lived in my father's house and was more as an older brother to us boys, than an uncle.

The great event of the year was the journey to Saratoga County, where we spent the summer vacation with our grandmother.

The start was made in the good steamboat, Isaac Newton, the jangle of whose starting bell seems still to ring in my ear. The crowded steamboat, the hurrying passengers, the state-room, the engine, and, as we travelled on, the moonlight on the palisades, and (I do not know but I may truthfully add) as the grand climax, the ice-cream man with his wine glasses of cream, then not so common as now,—all made a combination that just suited us boys. And Uncle Peter was the presiding genius of the occasion. Up in Saratoga County, there was that delight of children, a beautiful creek, flowing under the windows of my grandmother's house and the pleasure there was endless. The baths, though the water was sufficiently shallow to remove all danger of drowning, about up to our knees, and the dam we built and the mill-wheel that turned below it, made of two shingles crossed, and the fishes, finger-length, that we caught amid much excitement, all these brought out Uncle Peter in full force. Time passed, and we had to share our friend, of whom we claimed full proprietorship, with another. Uncle Peter was to be married. He married Aunt Minnie and settled down in 26th Street, New York, which then became our Mecca with very frequent pilgrimages. There was a circle of young friends that we would meet often at this house and very merry were the hours there.

The great feature was the Scotch songs that Aunt Minnie used to sing. I hear them yet, "Will ye no come back again," "Castles in the air," "Annie Laurie," "In the garb of old Gaul," "The Land of the Leal." We had never heard much singing in our own home. This was our first introduction to the world of song, and what a solace and inspiration to the heart of man is song! We boys owned its charm at once and always, like Oliver Twist, asked for more. And never was there a more willing singer. She did not have colds, nor was she of the number who cannot sing without their notes and never have their notes, nor did she require a special auditory. Boys were good enough for her, so away she went on another song and the applause was rapturous.

These evenings are my memory of Aunt Minnie, and it is one of the happiest memories of my life. Heaven is a tuneful place and I imagine she is enjoying it.

We met for the last time in the cars on

a sad errand, my brother's funeral. It was he and I that used to turn our steps so often to the 26th Street house. Our steps always turned together in those days, from the first day of schooling to the last of graduating at the Theological Seminary, fifteen years after. She and I both loved him very dearly, and as we sat in the same seat we talked of the one who was suddenly called away. She was the same eager, brimful one that she had always been, interested in everything, the old days or the present experience, and I little thought it was the last talk we would ever have on earth. And that is well, to move forward to the close in full flood, like a great river meeting the ocean; it is good to die so. God gave her long and happy years with her husband, God gave her a beautiful family of children, and her woman's heart was full.

NOT CHANGED BUT GLORIFIED.

BY P. T. M.

Not changed, but glorified! Oh beauteous language
      For those who weep,
Mourning the loss of some dear face departed,
      Fallen asleep!

Hushed into silence, never more to comfort
      The hearts of men,
Gone, like the sunshine of another country,
      Beyond our ken.

Will she be changed, so glorified and saintly,
      That we shall know her not?
Will there be nothing that shall say, "I love thee,
      And I have not forgot?"

O faithless heart, the same loved face transfigured
      Shall meet thee there,
Less sad, less wistful, in immortal beauty
      Divinely fair.

Let us be patient, we who mourn, with weeping,
>> Her vanished face,
The Lord has taken, but to add more beauty
>> And a diviner grace.

Think of us, dearest one, while o'er life's waters
>> We seek the land,
Missing thy voice, thy touch, and the true helping
>> Of thy pure hand.

Till through the storm and tempest, safely anchored
>> Just on the other side,
We find thy dear face looking through death's shadows,
>> Not changed, but glorified.

www.ingramcontent.com/pod-product-compliance
Lightning Source LLC
Chambersburg PA
CBHW021946160426
43195CB00011B/1244